INCREDIBLE INVENTIONS

600

FACT ATTACK

INCREDIBLE INVENTIONS

Ian Locke

MACMILLAN CHILDREN'S BOOKS

First published 1999
by Macmillan Children's Books
a division of Macmillan Publishers Ltd
25 Eccleston Place, London SW1W 9NF
and Basingstoke

Associated companies throughout the world

ISBN 0 330 37494 X

1 3 5 7 9 8 6 4 2

A CIP catalogue record for this book is available from
the British Library.

Printed by Mackays of Chatham plc, Chatham, Kent.

INCREDIBLE INVENTIONS

DID YOU KNOW THAT . . .

★ Beethoven composed the overture 'The Battle of Vitoria' in 1813 for a mechanical orchestra of 42 instruments invented by J. N. Maelzel.

★ The steel nib pen was only invented in 1803. Up to then the only practical writing instrument was a feather quill pen.

★ Jethro Tull invented the seed drill in 1701, allowing crops to be sowed in rows without wasting seed.

★ Clarence Birdseye discovered the process for his frozen food in Labrador. He put fresh vegetables in a bucket of water and then let them freeze solid. It took him about ten years to produce machinery that could imitate nature. Once this was done he established his frozen food company. His idea attracted the attention of the food company Postum and he sold out for $22 million in 1929. The first packs of Birdseye frozen food went on sale in 10 grocers in Springfield, USA, on March 6 1930.

★ In 90 years over 12 'nose picking' inventions have been filed in the USA.

★ The General Electric company invented fluorescent lighting in 1935 – it was green! Tube lights were first sold in three sizes and seven colours in 1938. The first fluorescent lights in Britain appeared on the westbound platform of the Piccadilly underground station in 1945.

★ There are many inventions where the inventor remains unknown. They include:

1. Spectacles.
2. The fork.
3. Glass windows.
4. Gunpowder.
5. The magnifying glass.
6. The glass mirror.
7. The wheel.
8. The bow and arrow.

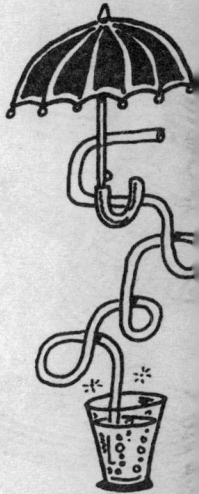

9. Lemonade. It was invented in Paris in 1630, using sugar from the West Indies.
10. The cuckoo clock.

★ 19-year-old Frenchman Blaise Pascal invented a machine to do sums in 1642 – it could add and subtract.

★ The first US patent was awarded on July 1 1790 to Samuel Hopkins.

★ At the age of 27, Eli Whitney invented the cotton 'gin' in the USA. It was the first change in cotton picking in over 2000 years. Its invention, in 1792, was to have a huge effect on American and European business and greatly increase the American use of slaves.

★ Christian Huygens of Holland invented the pendulum clock in 1656.

★ The American inventor of nylon, Wallace Carothers, was a shy and unsure man. He was working for the Du Pont chemical company when he discovered the chemical formula for nylon. The very first strand was squeezed out of a hypodermic needle in 1934. To start with, this first man-made fibre was used for toothbrushes and then stockings. Carothers had no idea how important his work was and he became depressed. He felt a failure and killed himself in 1937. In 1940 alone 36 million pairs of nylon stockings were sold!

★ James Watt became famous for the invention of the steam engine, but he also invented the first duplicating

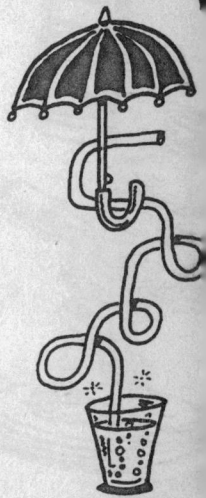

machine for business, in Birmingham in 1778. Despite his great success Watt had a fear for almost all his adult life of being broke.

★ It was German art publisher Rudolph Ackerman who first thought up the gears which were, almost 100 years later, used for the first motor cars.

★ The modern penny in the slot machine was invented by Englishman Colonel John Sanderman. His family remains famous for its drink, port, but he also made history in another way – he took part in the successful Charge of the Heavy Brigade in the Crimean War.

★ Levi and Strauss came up with jeans in 1850. Though first made with canvas, another cloth was needed for hard

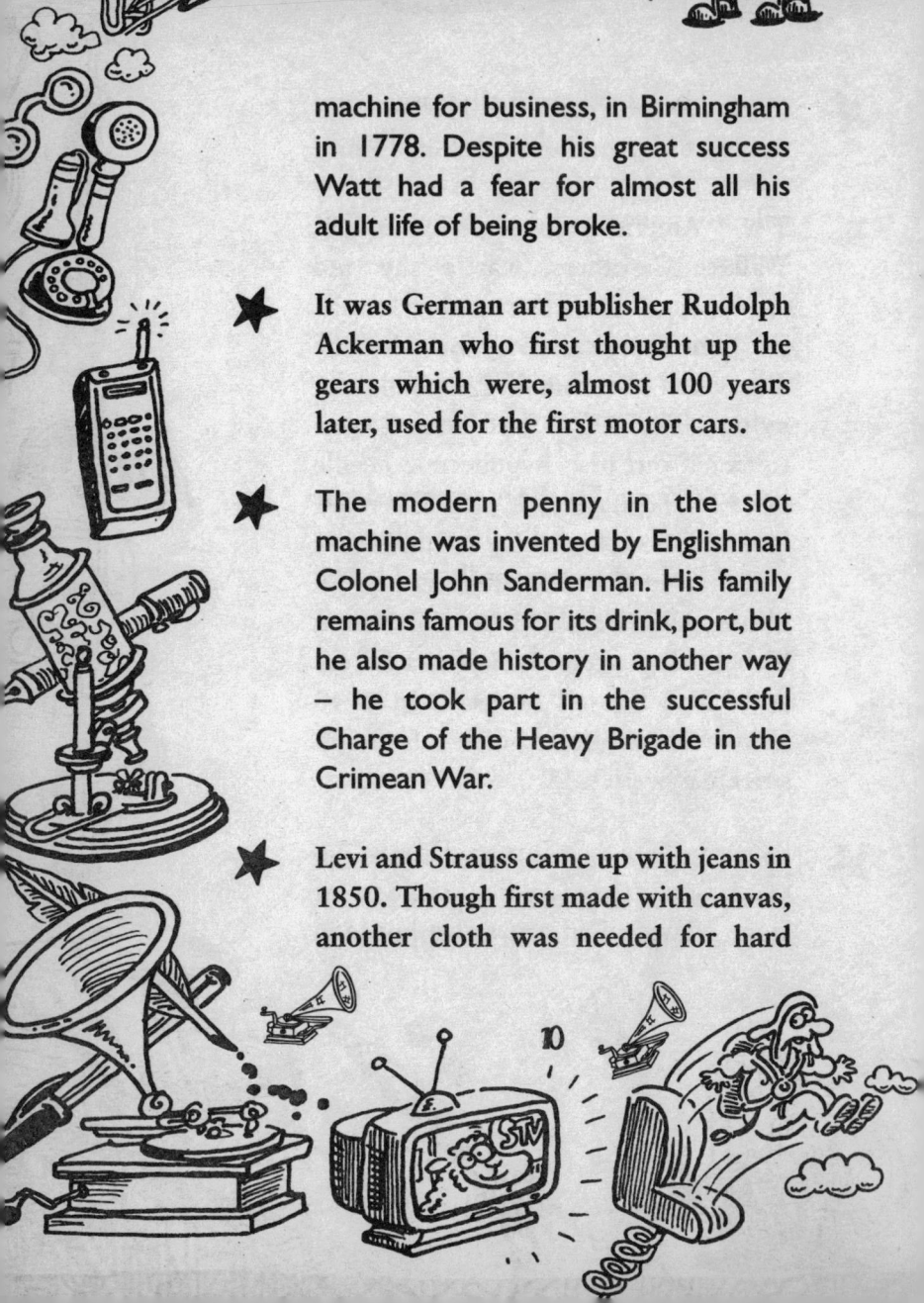

wear. This cloth originally came from Nîmes, France, so they were called *de Nîmes* or denims. They first went on sale to miners in San Francisco as 'bibless overalls'.

★ Isaac Singer, the American inventor who perfected the sewing machine, had 24 children.

★ An American Mr Bean invented the first orange crate in 1875. Just as useful was the cheap cardboard box – invented by Scottish-born Robert Gair in 1879.

★ Frederick Walton, of England invented and named 'linoleum' in 1860.

★ The cat flap was invented over 700 years ago! The famous scientist Sir Isaac Newton had one at his house in

London in the 1700s. The modern cat flap may have been invented by the British film star James Mason, who made a spring cat flap for his Hollywood home.

★ Frank Whittle spent years working on the jet engine while on leave from the RAF. In 1937 he had a breakthrough when he was able to test the first jet engine. The noise was so great that Whittle and his team had to move to an abandoned foundry near Rugby.

★ Hungarian professor Erno Rubik came up with a mind-boggling puzzle, the Rubik Cube, in 1974. When it went on sale in the 1980s, over 100 million were sold.

★ George Eastman's Kodak camera went on sale in the US in 1888 with the slogan 'You press the button, we do the rest'.

★ Three different people share the invention of television – the Americans Zworykin and Farnsworth and the Scot John Logie Baird. Neither Farnsworth or Baird were quite given the praise they deserved. John Logie Baird originally began his experiments when poor health made him give up his business of making boot polish and jam! He was the pioneer of colour television in 1939. The work of Farnsworth was only recognized in the 1930s.

★ English carpenter John Harrison started early as an inventor. In 1713 he first went in for a Government

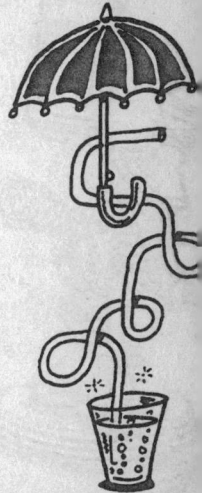

competition offering a £20,000 prize for the invention of an accurate chronometer, allowing sailors to know where they were. Two years later he produced his first invention, a clock with wooden wheels. After many years, in 1761, he came up with a remarkably accurate chronometer (to within one tenth of a second a day) and claimed the prize. It was only after he had appealed to the King, George III, that he was given the prizemoney.

★ Henry W. Avery's first aluminium saucepan was made in 1890 – his wife was still using it in 1933.

★ The first jet aircraft took off on August 27 1939 in Germany. It was designed by Dr Van Ohain.

★ The historian to Louis XV of France became the first human to leave the earth, on October 15 1783, in a Montgolfier balloon. The five-minute flight took him to 24 metres.

★ US patent 3,593,345 was awarded for a soundproofed toilet seat!

★ Francis Carley of Australia invented a 'tail light' for sheep, to protect them from attacks by the wild dog, the dingo.

★ That most useful of inventions, the safety pin, was invented in three hours by Walter Hunt in 1849. He had a $15 debt to pay off.

★ The first postcard was available in Britain on October 1 1870. The first picture postcard in England was of the

Eddystone Lighthouse. It was made for the Royal Naval exhibition of 1891.

★ Charles Darrow, an unemployed engineer, invented a game which he took to Parker Brothers in the US. They named it Monopoly and it first went on sale in 1935.

★ The Thermos flask was invented by Sir James Dewar. It was first sold by a German Reinhold Berger to help keep liquids hot.

★ The ejector seat was invented and developed by the British engineer James Martin, who died in 1981. The first tests of the seat were made with sandbags in May 1945. The first human used an ejector seat on July 24 1946.

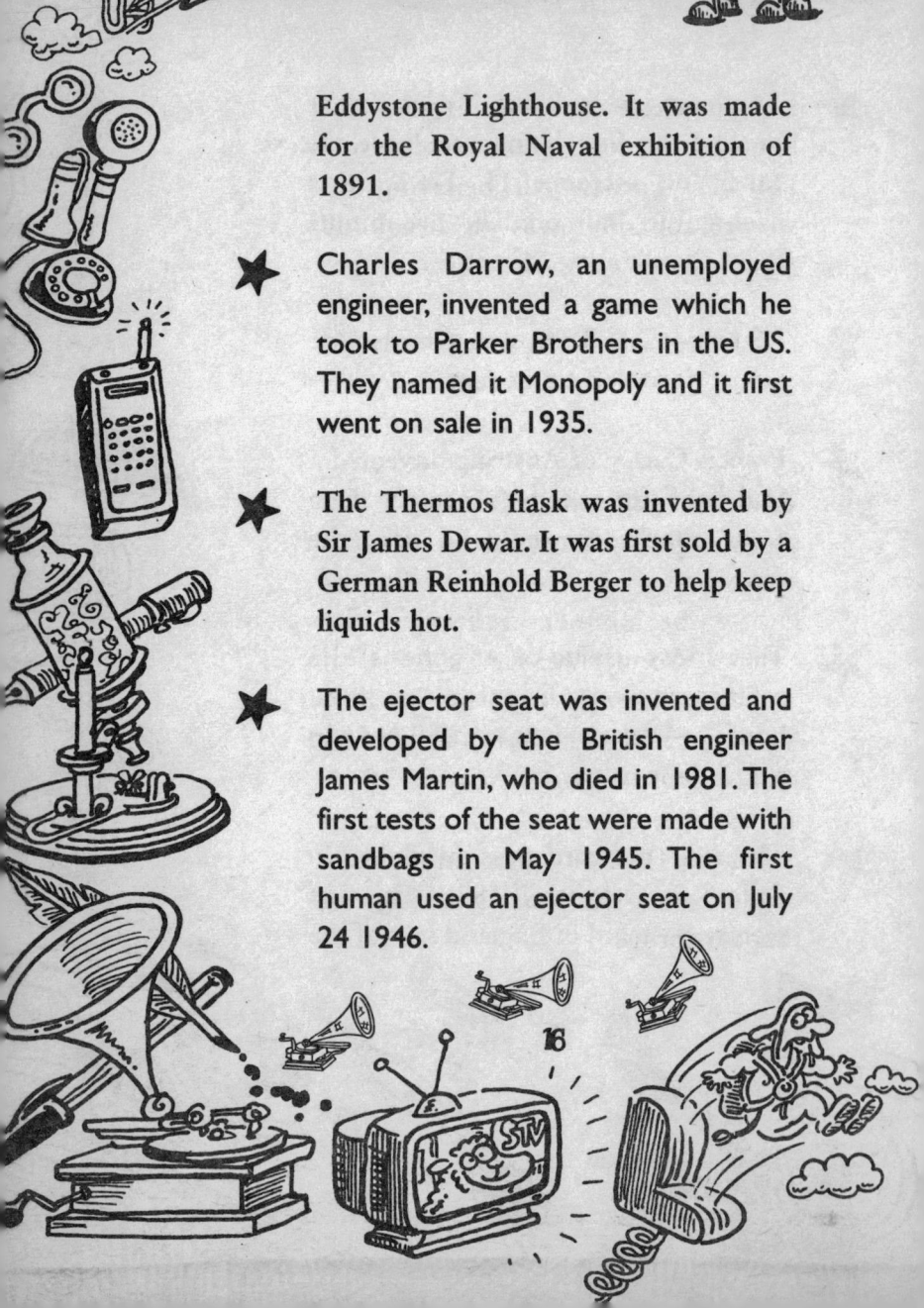

★ Los Angeles police once raided the home of the co-inventor of television Philo T. Farnsworth believing his strange apparatus was an illegal still for making alcohol! Another co-inventor, Baird, had a different problem. Among his first inventions were inflatable soles for shoes – they burst.

★ William Moulton Marston, a US psychologist, invented the lie detector – the polygraph. He became better known for another creation – the cartoon Wonder Woman!

★ Sir Robert Watson-Watt devised the first effective radar system in 1935. The system helped win the Battle of Britain in 1940. His first experiments began when he was working on thunderstorms.

★ Hedy Lamar, the Hollywood film actress, was a secret inventor. In June 1941 she and composer George Autheil developed a communication system for submarines.

★ When the Swiss introduced the world's first wristwatch in 1790, it was described as 'a watch to be fixed as a bracelet'.

★ Henri Moissan, a French chemist, tried to make artificial diamonds. He came up with something entirely different — calcium carbide which, in water, produced acetylene. This was the gas most commonly used in gas lights.

★ A German chemist Fritz Klatte invented the world's first plastic — vinyl chloride — by accident.

★ Legal registration of inventions, (patenting), is made each Tuesday at noon by the US Patent Office.

★ Two concert musicians, Leopold Godowsky and Leopold Mannes, invented the first colour film for use in an ordinary camera, in 1935. They paid for their experiments from their concerts until they found a backer in New York. After nine years they went to work at Kodak. The people there made fun of them, calling them 'those crackpots' – until they succeeded.

★ The first woman in the United States to be granted a patent (to protect her invention) was Mary Kies, of Killingley, Connecticut, on May 5 1809. She invented a device for 'weaving straw with silk or thread'.

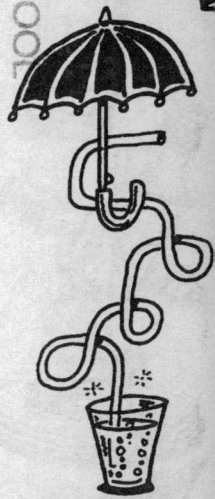

★ André Garnerin of Paris put together the first parachute and made a jump from 680 metres using a 7 metre diameter chute, supported by a wooden pole.

★ The man who invented canned foods, Nicolas Appert of France, was a chef and confectioner. Despite being praised for his invention and given the title 'Benefactor to Humanity' he died in poverty in 1841. He was also the inventor of the *bouillon* cube (known as the Oxo cube in Britain).

★ The US Wagner Typewriting machine company came up with a new form of the machine in 1897. They offered it to the Remington company. After looking at it Remington decided the machine 'couldn't replace a reliable and honest clerk' and turned it down.

Wagner was later sold to the Underwood company, who went on to sell 12 million of the new typewriters!

★ Italian physicist Alessandro Volta made the first electric battery in 1800.

★ Lawyer Henry D. Perky of Denver, US, invented Shredded Wheat. He called it the 'perfect food'.

★ British chemists invented the drug AZT for the company Wellcome in the late 1980s. It is thought that by the time the drug's patent runs out it will have earned $1 trillion!

★ The 'father of the computer' was Charles Babbage, an Englishman backed by the daughter of the poet Lord Byron, Lady Augusta Lovelace. He was unable to complete his

21

'analytical engine' after the Government withdrew money from the project. An early version of the machine was used by Babbage and Lady Lovelace for an 'infallible' system for betting on horses. It lost them a fortune. Among his other inventions was the speedometer.

★ There was an unusual producer for the first ever movie of Frankenstein — none other than US inventor Thomas Edison!

★ Dr John Kellogg, the American inventor of cornflakes, was a bit mad, though, to his credit, he also invented peanut butter. At one time he claimed 'Nuts may save the (human) race.' He didn't say what kind of nut.

★ The first machine gun used in war was operated by Confederate soldiers in the American Civil War at the Battle of Fairoaks, Virginia, in May 1862. It was called the Williams machine gun.

★ After the invention of barbed wire by the American Joseph F. Glidden in 1876, ranchers and farmers in Texas were not pleased to see the land dotted with it. One said 'I wish the man who invented barbed wire had it all wound round him in a ball and the ball rolled into hell.'

★ Charles N. Van Cleave invented the coin operated lock used on toilet doors in 1910.

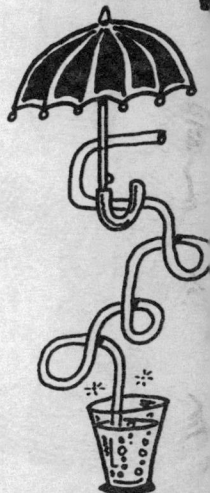

★ There was an invention for a mouse trap registered in the US. Not so different, you might think, except this one used lassoes to catch the mice!

★ The first typewriters were sold in the United States as a help for clergymen to save time when writing sermons.

★ For some time after the invention of the telephone people answered it by saying 'Ahoy'. It was the brilliant inventor Thomas Edison who suggested using 'Hello' instead.

★ Fed up with the state of the British roads, in 1815 John L. McAdam devised a new road surface of interlocking stones. Tar McAdam (tarmac) named after him, came later.

★ Machine guns, or rather machine bows, which fired 100-200 arrows a minute, were around in Ancient Greece and Rome.

★ Taximeters were included on Roman carriages.

★ While Thomas Edison had over 1,100 inventions to his name, Samuel Morse had only one – the telegraph.

★ In 1910 a Mr O'Sullivan was annoyed by the vibration of the machines in the American factory where he worked. To solve the problem he brought in a rubber mat. But someone else had their eye on it and it disappeared. O'Sullivan could only find a small piece of rubber, so he cut it to fit the heels of his shoes — inventing the rubber sole.

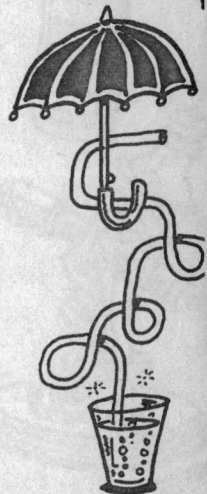

★ Frenchman M. Monier threw his flowerpots about when angry. After breaking a number of them he found this expensive. He thought he'd try to make his own, using wire mesh and concrete. It worked – they didn't break, and he'd also invented ferro concrete. This became the basic metal mesh and concrete mix used for bridges, skyscrapers and other buildings.

★ James Watt, the Scots inventor of the steam engine and one of the most important people in the history of invention, was thought lazy and not very bright when he was young. His aunt complained he spent too much time taking the lid off a kettle, then putting it back on again, and playing about with the steam!

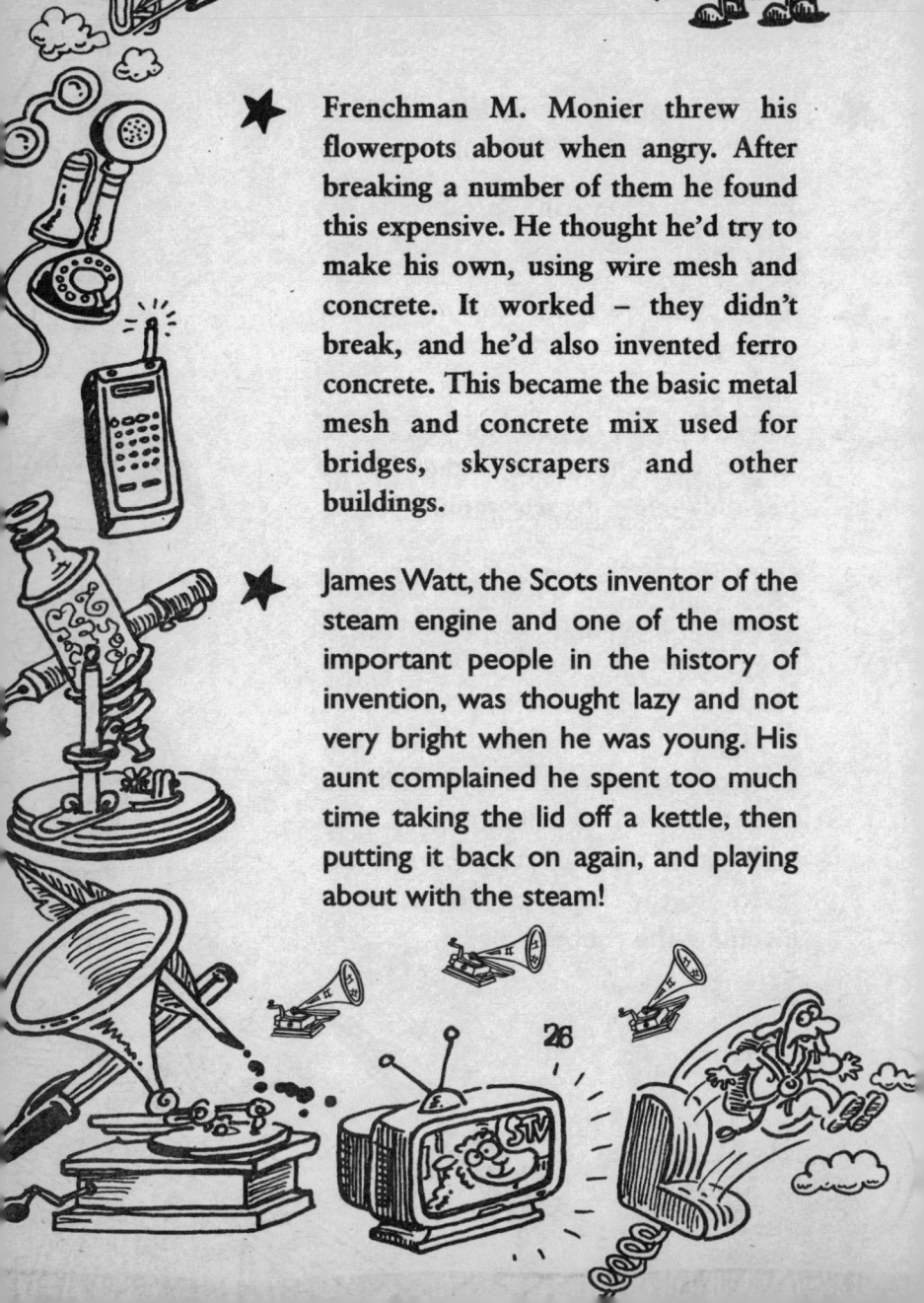

⭐ Inventions linked to the original inventor or manufacturer.

1. The mackintosh, produced by Charles Macintosh in 1823. No one knows where the extra K came from.
2. Morse Code. Invented by Samuel Morse of the USA.
3. The Hoover. Named after the man who first manufactured the upright electric vacuum cleaner.
4. The saxophone. Invented by Antoine Sax of Belgium in 1841.
5. The Bunsen burner. Named after the German chemist/inventor Robert Bunsen.
6. The Davy Lamp. Invented by Sir Humphry Davy.
7. The Yale lock. Invented by Linus Yale in the US in 1865.

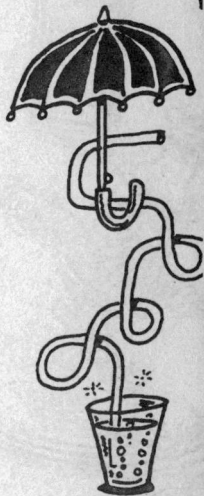

★ Portland cement is the basic material for all modern buildings. It was invented by Joseph Aspdin of Leeds in 1824, using limestone and clay which is ground up and burned.

★ The photo film roll was invented by David Houston of Wisconsin and patented on October 11 1881.

★ George Stephenson built the world's first railway between Stockton and Darlington in 1825. The trains ran regularly.

★ Samuel B. Morse, the American artist, developed the idea of the telegraph while on board the ship Sully, sailing from England to America. His first message was 'What Has God Wrought?' sent from the offices of the US Supreme Court in Washington to

28

his partner Alfred Vail in Baltimore on May 24 1844. Morse is the only famous inventor to have a picture exhibited at the Royal Academy in London.

★ When the great French film pioneer Georges Méliès was asked to sell his invention of cinema to one of the Lumière brothers, the old man refused. He told Lumière, 'Young man, you should thank me. This invention is not for sale, but if it were it would ruin you . . . It has no commercial future'! The Lumière brothers went on to give the world's first public showing of a film on December 28th 1898.

★ The coin-operated pay telephone was invented in 1889.

The American musician Les Paul was once involved in a car crash. While in hospital he thought up the idea of an electric guitar which he called the 'log'. When he had made it, he sold the idea to Gibson, and the first Gibson Les Paul electric guitar went on sale in 1952.

Simon Ingersoll invented the pneumatic rock drill in the USA in 1871. It has not changed much in 150 years.

Nicholas Tesla, who died in 1943, was one of the most important, but strangest inventors ever. Among his great inventions were the fluorescent light, the modern transformer, the modern power station, large elements of radio and aerial antenna. He spent almost all his life alone,

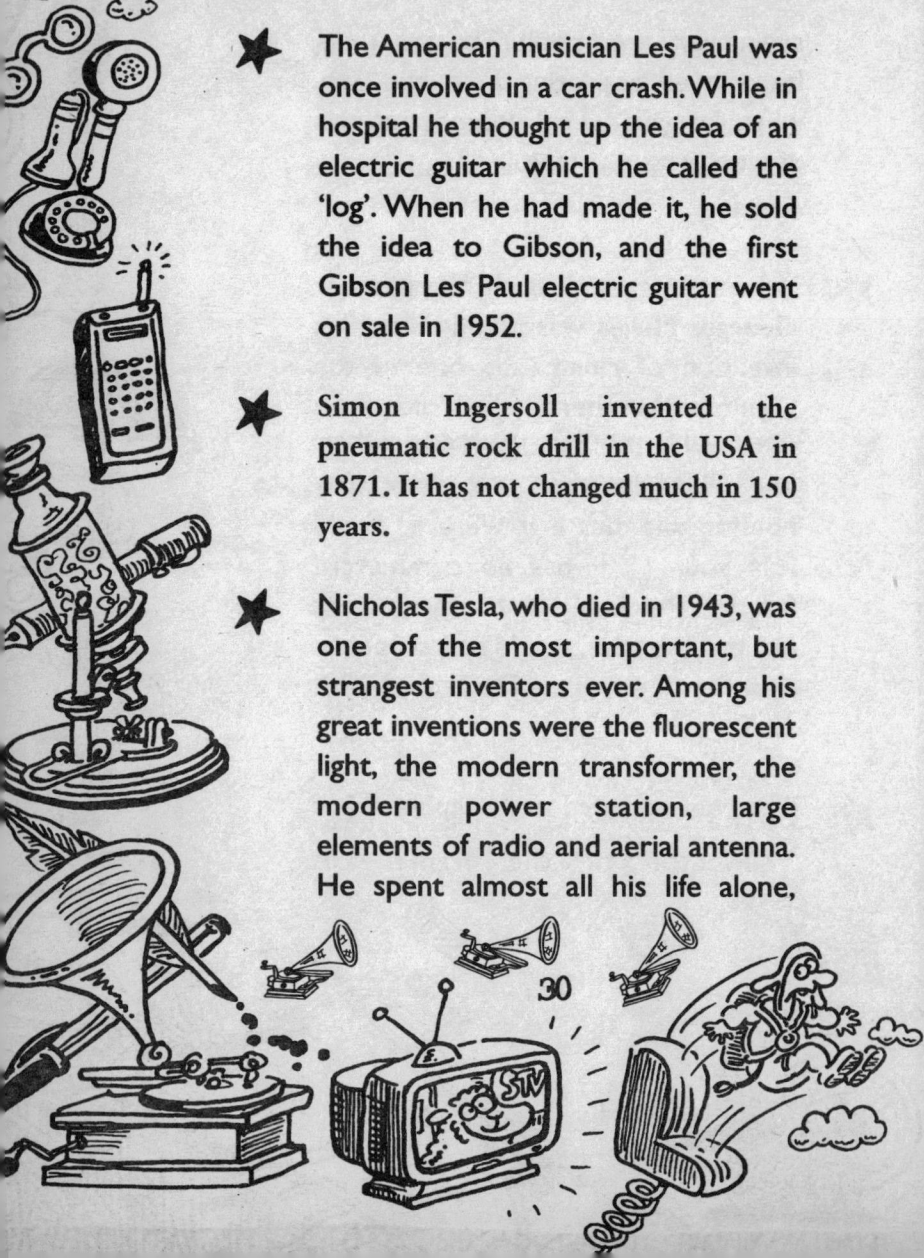

seeing very few people. The only time he enjoyed appearing in public was when he gave weird demonstrations of electricity on stage.

★ At the age of only 30, Edison made the world's first recording, on December 6 1877; it was of Mary Had a Little Lamb.

★ Vicars and priests seemed rather good at invention. Among them have been:

1. The Reverend William Fisken, inventor of the steam plough and central heating for churches.
2. The Reverend Edmund Cartwright, inventor of the power loom.
3. The Reverend William Lee, inventor of the frame for

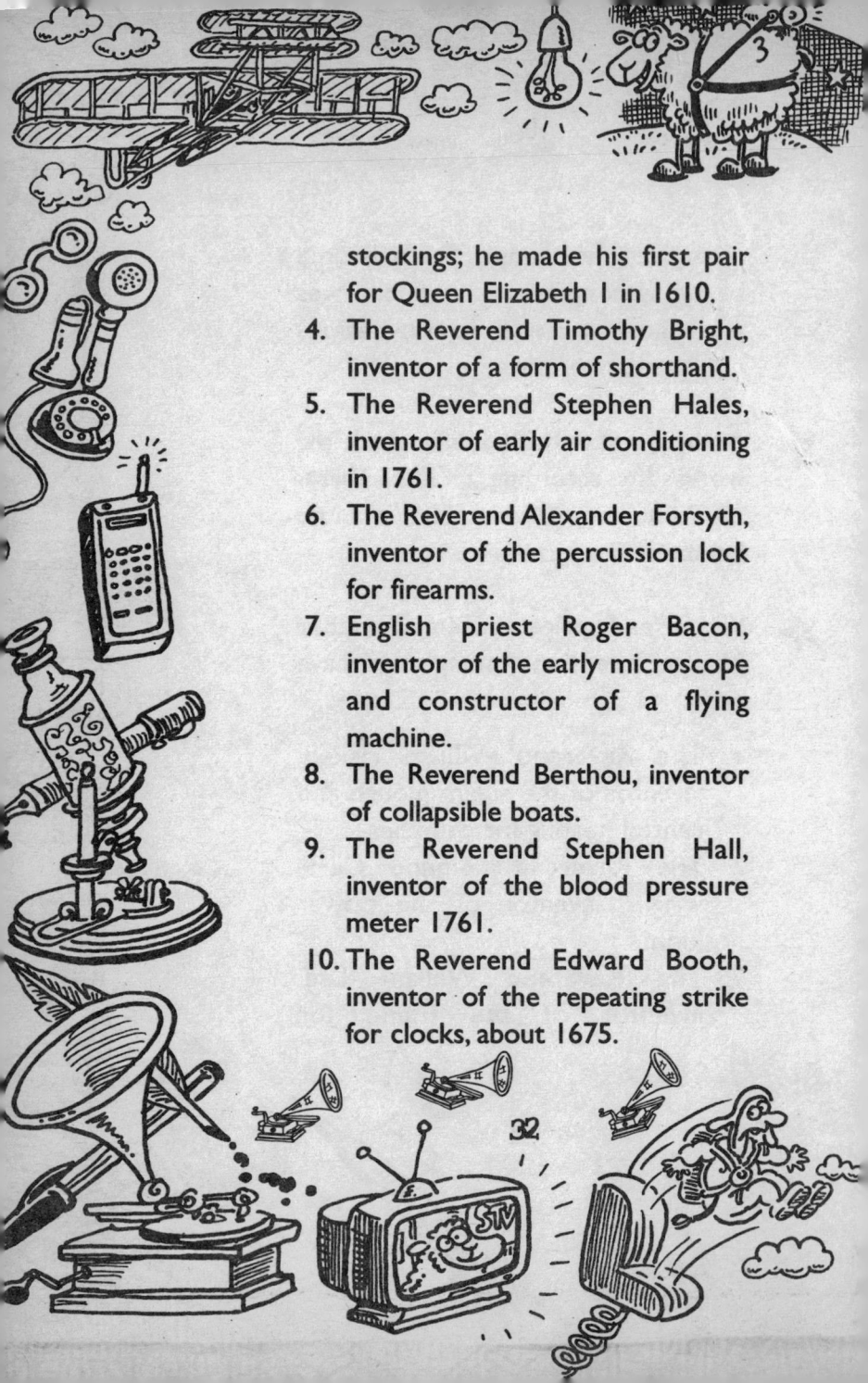

stockings; he made his first pair for Queen Elizabeth I in 1610.

4. The Reverend Timothy Bright, inventor of a form of shorthand.

5. The Reverend Stephen Hales, inventor of early air conditioning in 1761.

6. The Reverend Alexander Forsyth, inventor of the percussion lock for firearms.

7. English priest Roger Bacon, inventor of the early microscope and constructor of a flying machine.

8. The Reverend Berthou, inventor of collapsible boats.

9. The Reverend Stephen Hall, inventor of the blood pressure meter 1761.

10. The Reverend Edward Booth, inventor of the repeating strike for clocks, about 1675.

★ Kirkpatrick Macmillan, a Dumfries blacksmith, invented the first bicycle in 1809. The wheels were 32 inches in front, and 42 inches at the rear. He had a carved horse's head on the front of the wooden frame.

★ For the man who invented so much to do with communications, Edison was a bit weird. He preferred to read in Braille rather than print and when he proposed to his first wife, he used Morse Code!

★ Printed and gummed stamps were the idea of June Longeville, the lady in waiting to Louis XVI. The world's first adhesive stamps went on sale on May 1 1840 in Britain, they were printed by the US inventor Jacob Perkins. UK stamps are the only ones

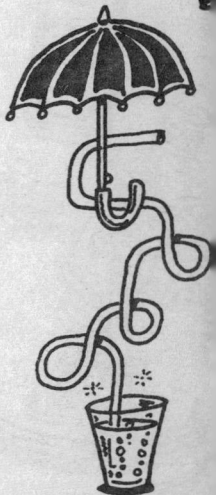

in the world without the name of the country of issue on them.

★ The co-inventor of photography, Joseph Niepce of France, took six hours to take his first photo, in 1827.

★ The mouth organ was invented in Germany in 1821.

★ German Karl Benz developed the first petrol-driven motorized vehicle, a tricycle, in 1878.

★ The explosive nitroglycerine was first made in Italy in 1847. The results were so horrifying to the inventor Sobrero that he forgot about it. Alfred Nobel rediscovered the process some 20 years later, developed a stable form, dynamite, and made his fortune.

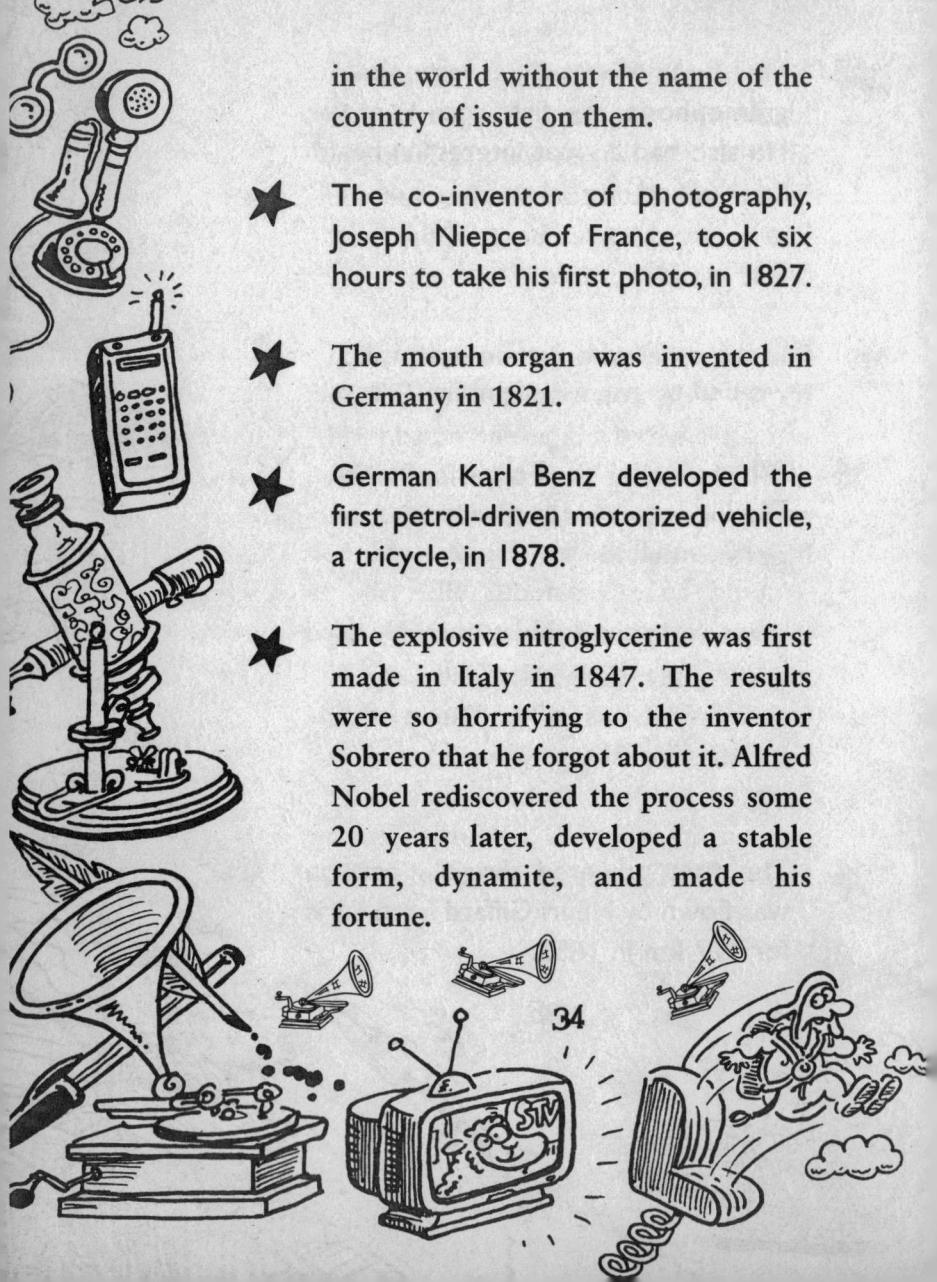

★ Emil Berliner was the inventor of the gramophone, the first record player. He also had a great interest in health and helped introduce bug-free milk and dairy products in the US. He always believed women were very good at science and gave a large part of his fortune to encourage girls and women to go into scientific research.

★ When living in Belfast, vet John Dunlop invented the pneumatic tyre in 1878 so that his 10-year-old son would have a smooth bike ride to school over the cobblestones. He used a rubber sheet and strips of linen from an old dress belonging to his wife. The tyres were at first made fun of, being known as 'pudding tyres'.

★ The first powered dirigible balloon was flown by Henri Giffard from Paris for 127 km in 1852.

★ A US customs man, Gail Borden, played an important part in the US Civil War of 1860-65. His invention of condensed milk and concentrated foods may well have helped the Union army win the war.

★ The inventor and businessman Alfred Nobel is remembered by the Nobel prize. His father also has a place in history — he invented plywood.

★ The world's first escalator was put into the Old Iron Pier at Coney Island, near New York, in 1896. It had been invented by Jesse Reno of New York.

★ Sometimes an accident can be helpful. When he was young, Englishman Joseph Bramah had an accident which stopped him becoming a farmer. After trying a

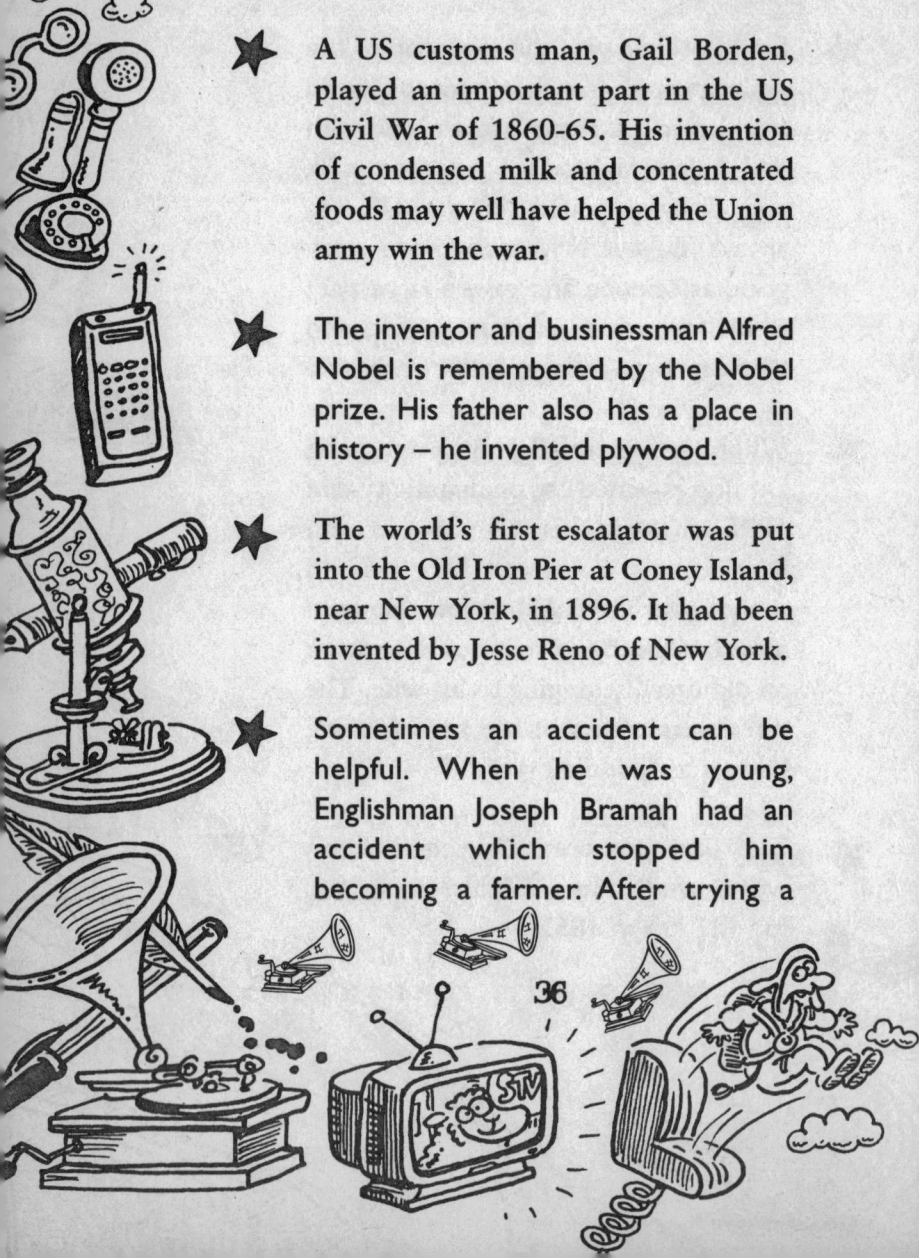

number of jobs, he became an inventor. He first became famous for a pickproof doorlock, then went on to invent a number of machines, including those for making paper and putting numbers on banknotes. He was also the man who thought up the idea of putting propellors on ships. He is said to have walked to London with his lock. He then held a competition offering £200 to anyone who could open it. The winner took 51 hours non-stop!

★ Dr Alexander Wood of Edinburgh invented the hypodermic syringe in 1853. It was immediately useful, but it soon caused problems – during the US Civil War of 1860-65 some 400,000 American soldiers used it to take drugs.

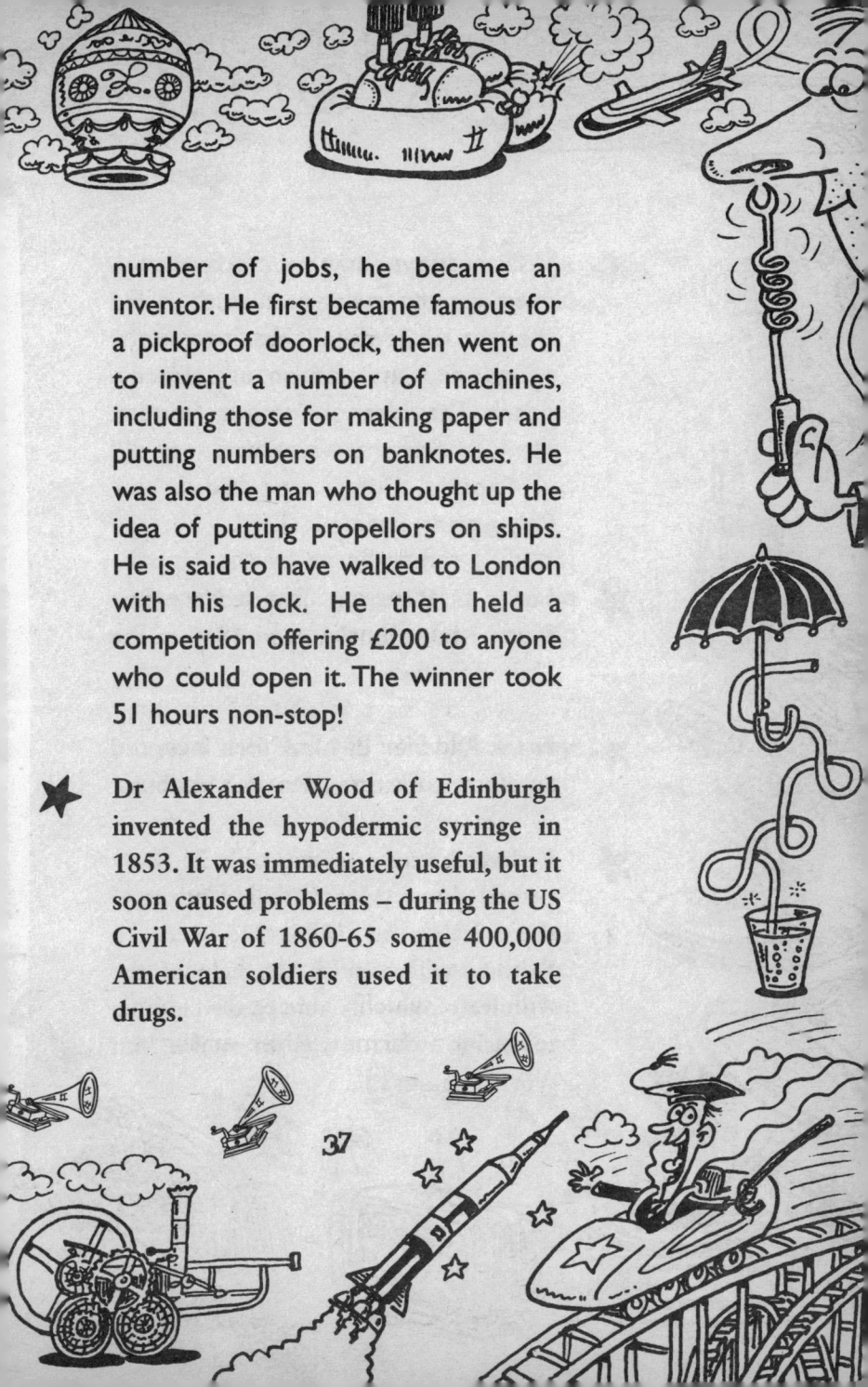

★ William Hoyng is now credited with inventing the modern surfboard. He thought it up while it was too windy to go into the sea on a California beach. The idea of using a wooden plank to ride the waves was very old – Captain Cook reported seeing Polynesians surfing in 1771.

★ James L. Plimpton invented the first four-wheel rollerskates in 1863 in the United States.

★ Frank Rancher of New York invented an electric exterminator for bedbugs.

★ Perhaps because he was only 21, Italy turned down Marconi's invention of the wireless in 1895. He went to Britain, where, with the help of the Admiralty, he was able to develop his invention which was to make him world famous.

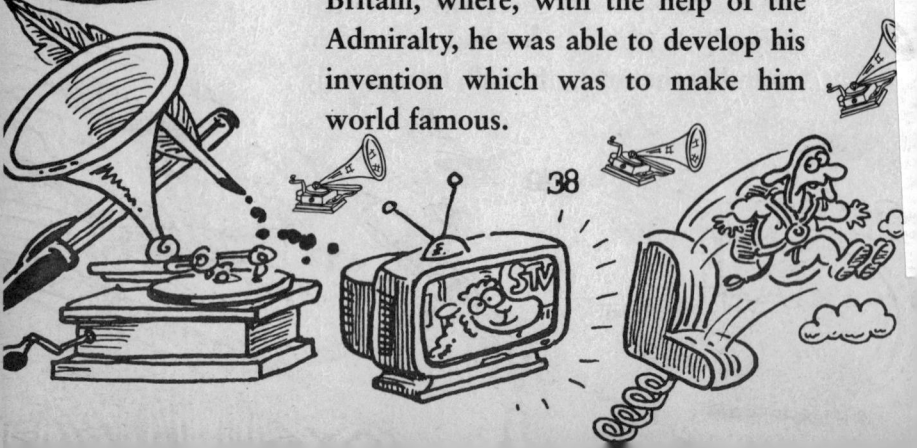

★ Louis Daguerre discovered fixed photographs by accident. He found that one of his glass plates was developed when he accidentally spilled mercury onto it.

★ When the choc ice, invented by Christian Nelson in the US, first came to Britain in June 1926, it was called 'something in the nature of a miracle'.

★ The coffee percolator was invented by James H. Nason of Franklin, Massachusetts, US in 1865.

★ Alexander Graham Bell's first words on his telephone were not quite what history expected. They were 'Mr Watson, come here, I want you.' It wasn't as though he had history in mind at the time; after all, he was only

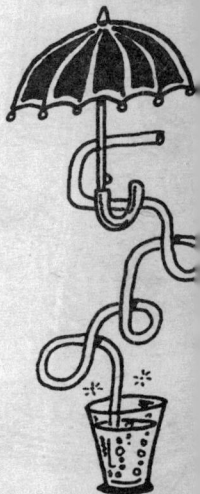

29. He beat Elisha Gray in filing his patent for the telephone by three hours, in 1876; it was Bell's birthday. Queen Victoria first used the telephone in 1878.

★ Benjamin Franklin, the great 18th-century American politician, thinker, scientist and publisher, was also an inventor. Among his inventions were bifocal spectacles, the rocking chair and the lightning rod.

★ Richard Trevithick, the British inventor, was the first to use a steam engine for a railway, some 25 years before Stephenson. His road loco carried passengers for the first time on Christmas Eve 1801. He used a steam loco on a track in London in 1808. His efforts were unsuccessful and he died penniless. One of the passengers

was, however, George Stephenson, who took notes and later used them for his own ideas for steam locos.

★ Bette Nesmith-Graham came up with a correcting fluid for typing mistakes in 1956. She called it Mistakes Out. She tried to interest the giant typewriter and computer company IBM in her invention, but they turned her down. As a result she began making it herself, changing the name to Liquid Paper. Though she made a name for herself, her son, Mike, became more famous — he was a member of the 1960s chart-topping band The Monkees.

★ The Dot and Dash in Morse Code remember the names of the two children of one of Samuel Morse's supporters — the 13th President of the

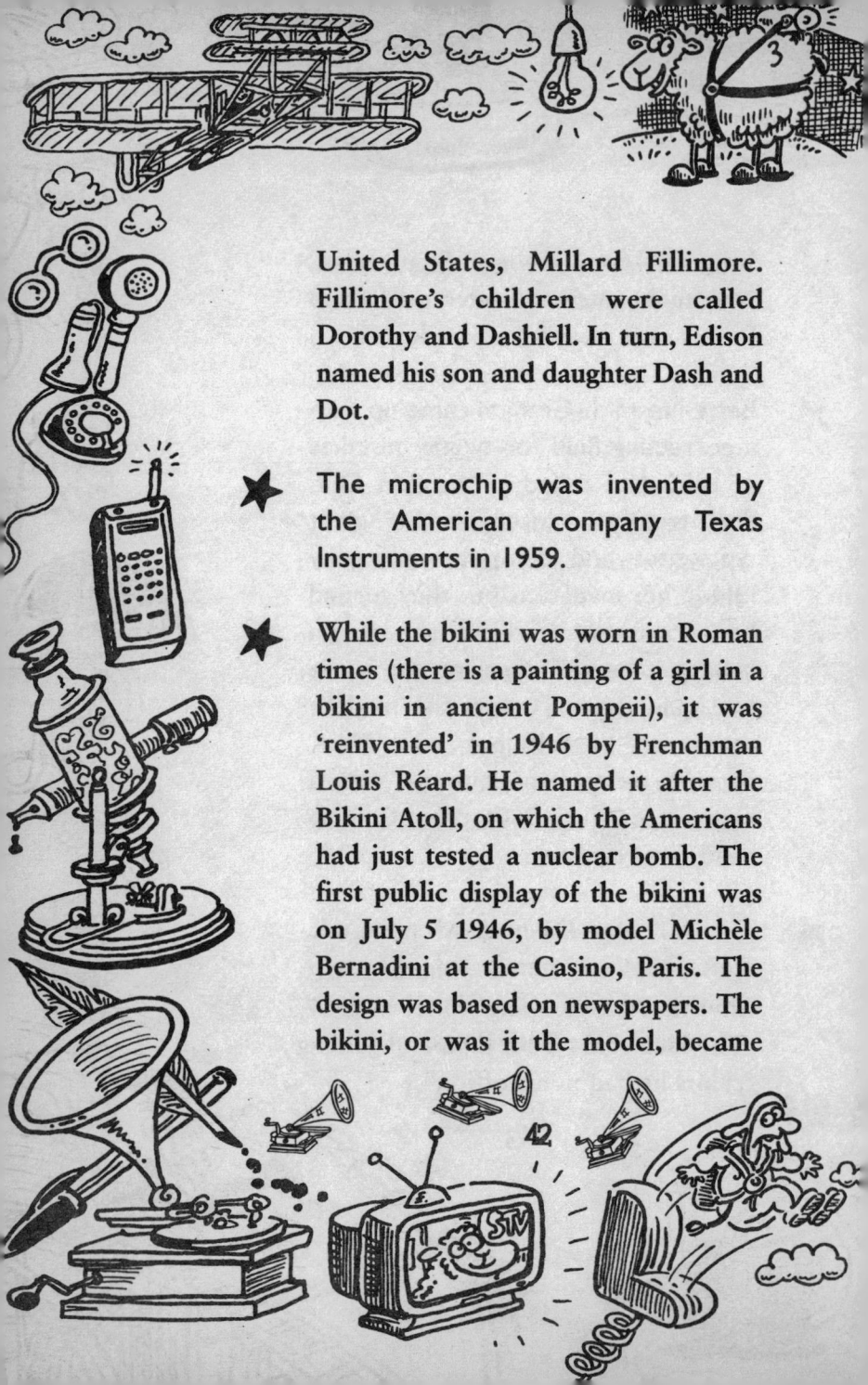

United States, Millard Fillimore. Fillimore's children were called Dorothy and Dashiell. In turn, Edison named his son and daughter Dash and Dot.

★ The microchip was invented by the American company Texas Instruments in 1959.

★ While the bikini was worn in Roman times (there is a painting of a girl in a bikini in ancient Pompeii), it was 'reinvented' in 1946 by Frenchman Louis Réard. He named it after the Bikini Atoll, on which the Americans had just tested a nuclear bomb. The first public display of the bikini was on July 5 1946, by model Michèle Bernadini at the Casino, Paris. The design was based on newspapers. The bikini, or was it the model, became immediately popular – she received 50,000 letters.

★ The world's first commercial computer was the British Ferranti Star, produced in 1950.

★ The shoelace was invented in 1790. Laces were to replace buckles on shoes.

★ Melville Bissell invented the carpet sweeper in his crockery shop in Grand Rapids, Michigan, in 1876 in an attempt to cure his allergy to the dust from the straw his china goods were packed in.

★ Syvan Goldman, who owned a supermarket in Oklahoma city, invented the shopping trolley in 1937. The idea came from a pair of folding chairs he had in his office.

★ Orville Wright who, with his brother invented the first heavier than air powered flying machine, was expelled from school in 1883. Their historic flight took place at Kitty Hawk on December 17 1903. Only two US newspapers bothered to cover the story.

★ Americans were first told about an IBM computer called Bessie, used during World War II, in 1950. Among other things, it had been used to investigate electric cannon the Nazis were said to be building, and helped with the atom bomb. Britain kept the existance of their own computer Colossus, used for code-breaking, a secret until the 1970s.

★ It's a beauty. Chester Carlson invented the Xerox photocopier in

1938. He developed the idea in the backroom of his mother's beauty salon in New York. One of the first copies he made was of his application for a patent.

★ Alexander Graham Bell was not idle after inventing the telephone. Not only did he begin the National Geographic magazine, he continued to experiment with kites, electricity, speedboats and machines for much of his life. One of the stranger jobs he did was to design a special metal detector to look for the bullet that hit US President James Garfield in 1881. Unfortunately the bedsprings of the bed on which the dying President lay interfered with the machine, and the location of the bullet could not be determined.

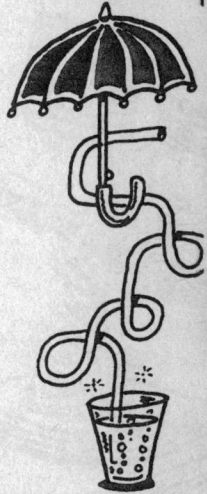

45

★ The cash dispenser was invented by John Shepherd-Barron and the first was opened at Barclays Bank in Enfield on June 27 1967.

★ In-line skates (Rollerblades) were first invented by a man who sold fruit in Piccadilly, London, R. J. Tyers, as long ago as 1823!

★ The inventor of the biro, Hungarian Laszlo Biró, hypnotist and journalist, had no money and didn't seem to be that interested in his invention. The first biro was made in Argentina and went on sale in 1944 at $40. In 1947 he gave up interest in the biro and went off to become a painter.

★ Bill Gates and Paul Allen, the founders of the US software company

Microsoft, invented BASIC, the computer language, in 1975. It stands for Beginners' All-Purpose Symbolic Instruction Code. By 1998 Bill Gates was reckoned to be the most wealthy man who ever lived.

★ John Julius of Australia invented the totalizer (Tote) machine for betting at racecourses in 1913.

★ Henry Ford introduced mass production for his car, the Model T, in 1904. The whole car could be built in 93 minutes by 1914. A popular song about Ford was written and became a hit in America; it was called 'The Flivver King'.

★ Frenchman Louis de Corlieu invented the flippers for use underwater in 1927.

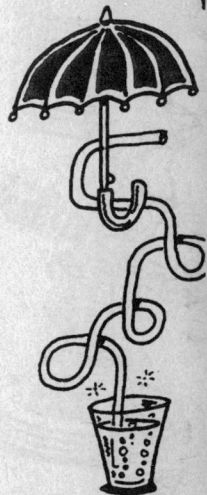

★ Journalist Arthur Wynne invented the crossword puzzle in New York in 1914.

★ William C. Loughlin has a reputation for imaginative 'expensive' inventions – a 'champagne' bottle that breaks easily and contains little champagne, for launching ships, and a 'millionaire's confetti' made of shredded banknotes.

★ Venetian blinds were patented by Edward Betan in London in 1769.

★ The modern hearing aid was invented by New Yorker Miller Hutchinson in 1901. The Queen of Edward VII, Alexandra, wore one during the Coronation of 1902 so she could hear what was going on.

★ American Charles Goodyear wanted to find rubber which would be useful in hot weather and at high temperature. One day, finishing work on his experiments, he dusted off some rubber and sulphur from his hands. It fell onto a hot stove. The rubber melted into a ball and reacted with the sulphur to create a new form of rubber. This vulcanized rubber was to solve his problem and be the solution to the making of millions of car tyres, among other products.

★ Australian woman inventor Sister Kenney, a nurse, was most unusual. After inventing a revolutionary stretcher for patients, she used the money she made to fund a large number of clinics to tackle the disease polio throughout the world.

★ The first electronic watch was made by the US Hamilton watch company in 1956. The battery was one supplied to the US military.

★ The inventor of yellow lines on roads was Bill Hadfield. He was paid only £2 for the idea by Greenwich council. Fifty years after he invented them he was caught on one. Bill did manage to make money, though, when he died aged 89, he left over half a million pounds in his will.

★ French sea captain M. Le Bris always wanted to fly. In 1857 he built a huge glider, with a 7 metre wingspan which looked like an albatross. He launched what he called his 'bird' from a farm cart. It made one short glide before crashing. He then abandoned the

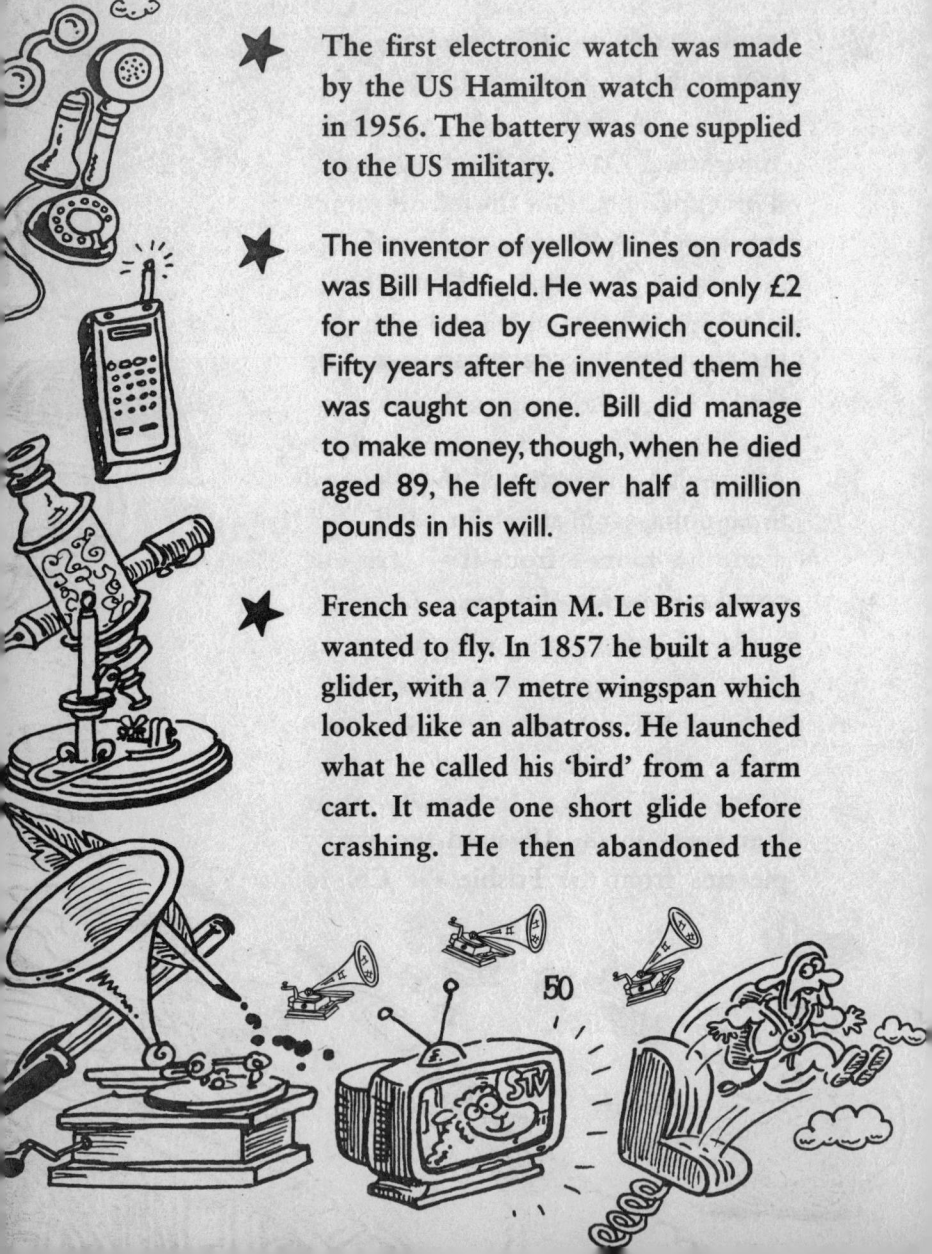

whole project after finding he'd broken his leg.

★ The Bath Oliver health biscuit was thought up by Dr William Oliver as he lay dying in his Mineral Water Hospital in Bath in the 1760s. To be sure it would be made, he dictated the recipe to his coachman before he died.

★ Although Volvo invented the standard three-point car seat belt in 1959, they made no money from it – everyone could use the idea for free.

★ The manual dishwasher was invented as long ago as 1855.

★ From the 1870s, students at Yale University in the US used the empty pie tins from the Frisbie Pie Co. to

throw to each other. It was not until 1948 that Fred Morrison took up the idea and produced what he called Morrison's Flyin' Saucer. The name was later changed to the Frisbee.

★ Dr Klaes Maertens and a student friend, Dr Herbert Funck, developed the Doc Marten boot from old tyres in 1947. The first pairs were made from sponge rubber and material used to repair aircraft. Doc Martens were made in Britain by R. Greggs and Co. of Wollaston, Northants, from April 1960.

★ The French company L'Oréal introduced the first mass-produced shampoo in 1934; it was called Dop.

★ Sometimes there are things which appear to have been around for ever,

but are really not that old. Among these inventions are:

1. The gymslip. Invented by Madame Bergman Osterburg of Sweden in 1892.
2. Toilet paper. Though probably invented by Joseph C. Gagetty in 1857 and sold as Gagetty's Medicated Paper, it only came into mass use in 1892.
3. Hot drinks vending machine. Invented in 1886.
4. The gumshield for boxers. Invented by a London dentist, Jack Marks, in 1902.
5. Ice cream in tubs or batches. Invented in 1902.
6. Kitty litter. Invented by American Ed Lowe in 1947.
7. The first self-supporting trousers were invented by Briton

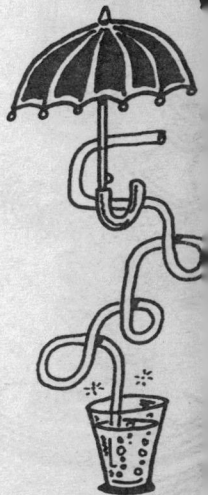

Alexander Simpson in 1934. He called them DAKS.

8. The flexible straw. Invented by Joseph B. Friedman in the USA in 1938.

9. The anorak. Invented in 1934.

10. Persil soap powder. Invented in 1907.

★ Louis Waterman, an insurance broker from New York, came up with the idea of a reliable fountain pen after messing up a document by spilling ink over it. His new pen was finished in 1884 and he began to make it in an old cigar shop, offering a guarantee of five years.

★ James I was the first English monarch to use a fork. The first picture of a fork appeared in the book *The Cooking Secrets of Pope Pius V* in 1570.

★ The aspirin tablet, invented by Karl Gerhardt in Germany in 1853, was first sold in 1915.

★ Garnet Carter, who owned Carter's Lookout Mountain Hotel, on the edge of the US Civil War battleground in Tennessee, laid out the first miniature golf course in 1927.

★ Percy Shaw, the inventor of Catseyes on roads, died aged 86 in 1976. He first thought of the idea when at night, the lights from his car were reflected in a cat's eyes. He had a fortune and owned a Rolls Royce, but had no curtains or carpets in his house. He had 4 TVs which he kept on a high volume all the time. He also insisted his factory was built round a sycamore tree he had climbed as a child.

⭐ The first electric kettle went on display at the World's Fair in Chicago in 1893.

⭐ John Koss began a company to make record players in Milwaukee in 1958. While working with headsets, he decided to try out stereo and came up with the world's first stereo headphones – they were held together with rubber hose and chicken wire!

⭐ Jacques Brandenberger, a Swiss man, spent a lot of time at his hobby – attempting to make machinery to produce the wrapping cellophane which he had invented. He suceeded in 1908, and made a fortune. He then retired to collect antiques.

★ Fish fingers went on sale for the first time in Britain on September 26 1955 in Southampton.

★ Samuel Crompton, who died in 1827, the inventor of the spinning mule, spent most of his life as a concert violinist. He was fated to be tricked out of the profit from his revolutionary invention.

★ 80 of the first sewing machines were destroyed by a mob in Paris in 1829. Britain had the same problem with machines. Mobs of people called 'Luddites' smashed them because they feared they would put them out of work.

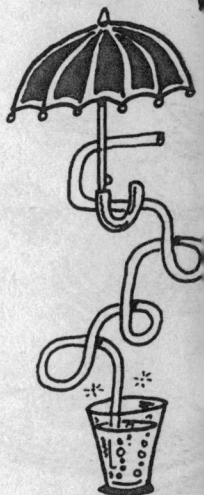

57

Sir Clive Sinclair has a string of inventions to his name – the first commercial pocket calculator, the pocket and wristwatch TV, the first major home computer and the C5, a bicycle-like vehicle powered by a washing machine motor (which was a failure). His ZX81 home computer alone sold over 1 million.

The US Air Force developed the infra-red camera in 1958. It was first tried out on a parking lot where cars which had been there for several hours before showed up on the developed film. Infra-red cameras can now be used to detect all sorts of action – even murder.

Daniel O'Connor and Herbert Faber invented a hard canvas-based surface in 1913 and called it Formica. The first

colour was black. By the 1960s a whole range of bright colours had been introduced, along with finishes like marble or wood.

★ As a result of the smooth work from the discovery to the making of nylon, the US company Du Pont was asked to make something very different – the atomic pile used to develop the first atom bomb.

★ It took the German Gutenberg seven years from 1448 to produce his 300 copies of the Bible with his new movable type. Each copy has 1282 pages.

★ Although Galileo is credited with the invention of the telescope, it was first made by the Dutchman Hans

Lippershey about two months before Galileo.

★ The musical toilet roll holder was patented by Richard Hardy in 1912.

★ Tetra Pak, the plastic-coated carton used for liquids and food, was invented by the Rausing brothers of Sweden. It was first shown to the public at the Royal Show in Nottingham in 1955.

★ The elastic band was invented by London rubber manufacturer Stephen Perry in about 1845.

★ The English priest Roger Bacon was a 13th-century scientist. He described the idea of the *camera obscura* (the first camera), and predicted the steamship, aeroplane and television.

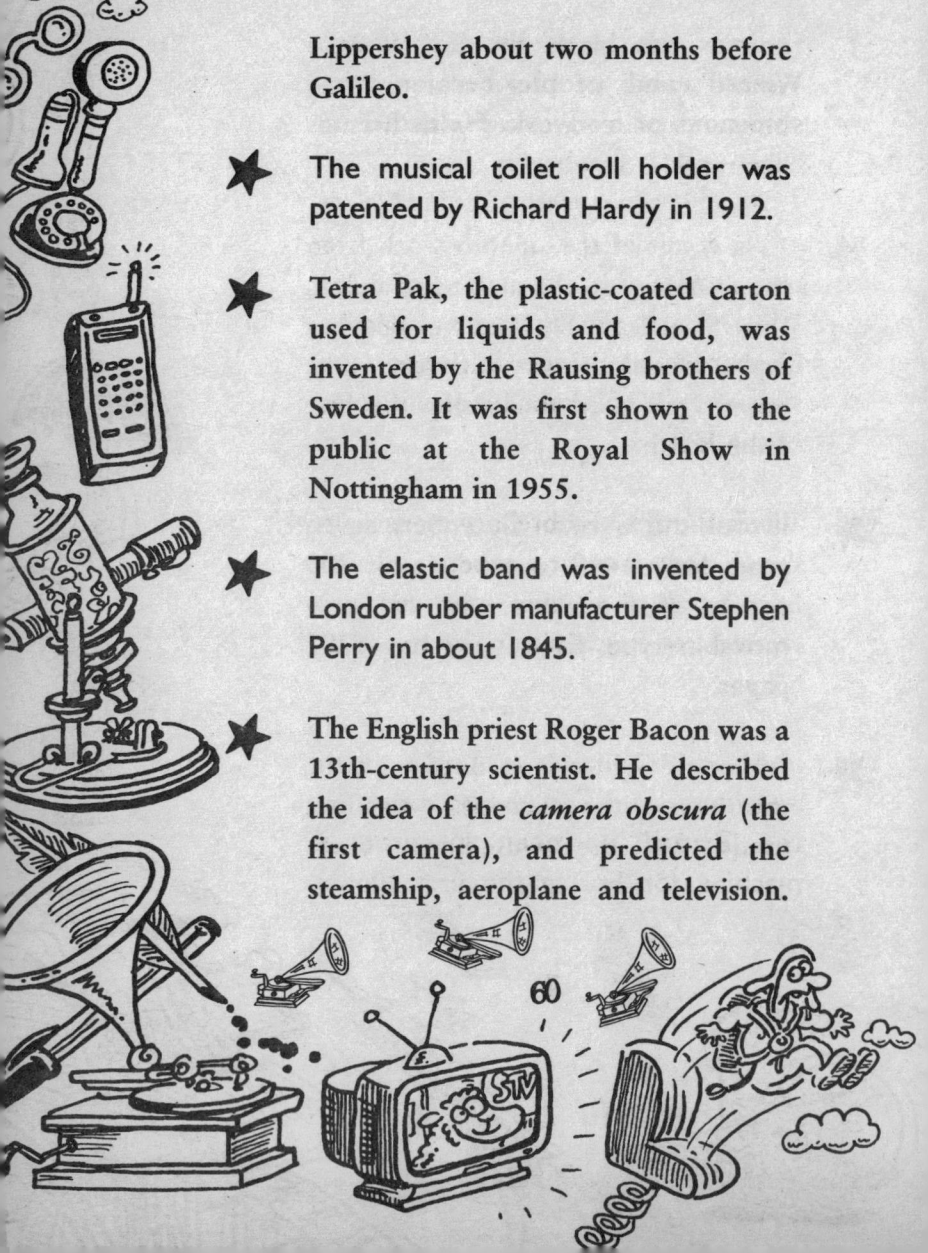

He was known as the 'Knowledge Wizard' and people became very suspicious of his work. He ended up being jailed for heresy from 1277-1292, dying two years after his release at the age of 80.

★ The first alarm clock was invented by Leonardo da Vinci. It woke the sleeper by a soft rubbing of the soles of the feet.

★ When the first umbrella was used in the United States, it was reported that horses bolted, women screamed and fainted and children went hysterical at the sight!

★ Inventions sometimes come from watching nature. Sir Isambard Brunel, the British engineer, invented a machine for boring the first tunnel

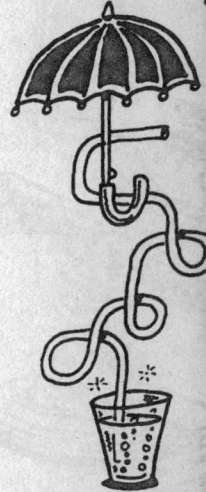

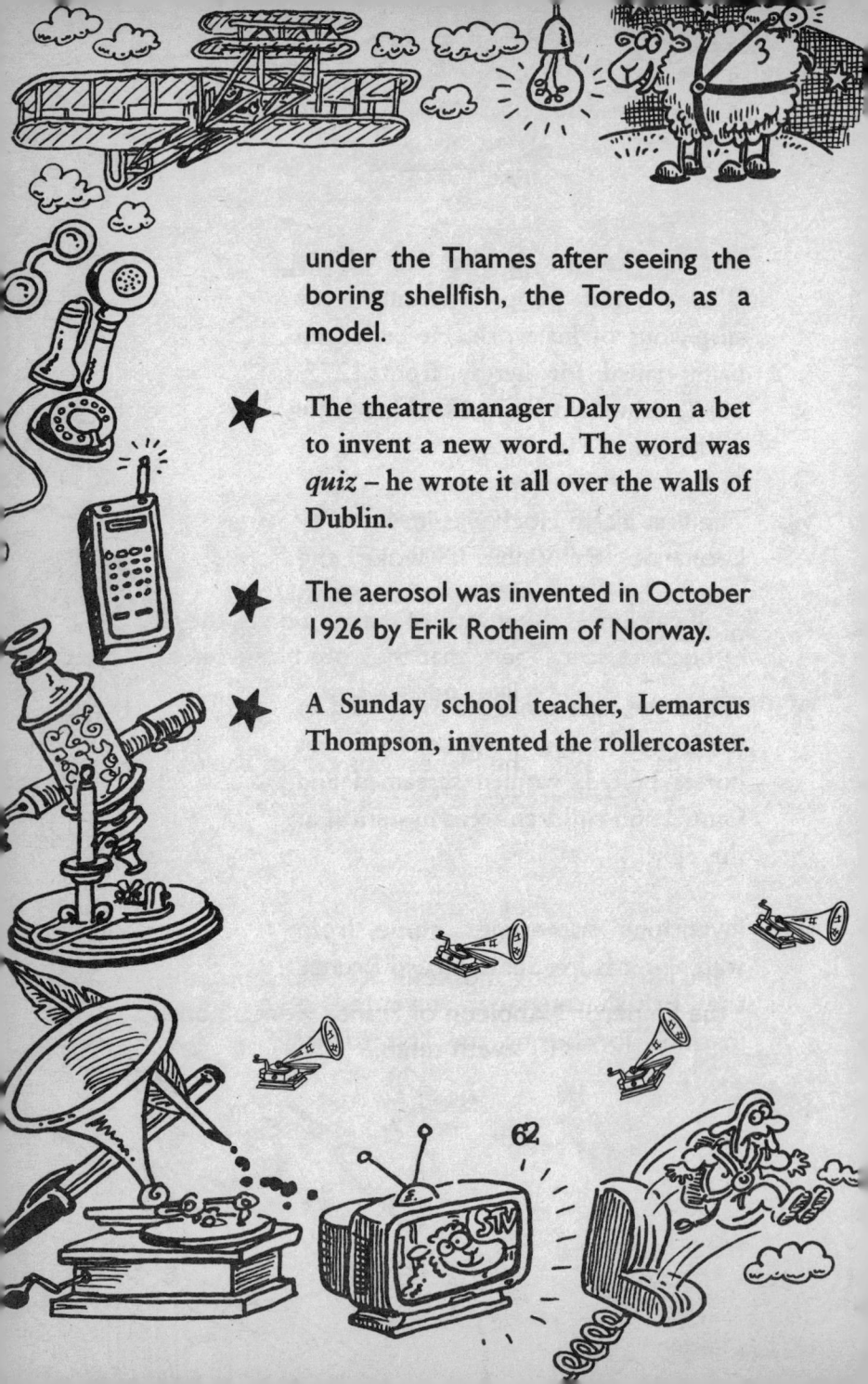

under the Thames after seeing the boring shellfish, the Toredo, as a model.

★ The theatre manager Daly won a bet to invent a new word. The word was *quiz* – he wrote it all over the walls of Dublin.

★ The aerosol was invented in October 1926 by Erik Rotheim of Norway.

★ A Sunday school teacher, Lemarcus Thompson, invented the rollercoaster.

DID YOU KNOW THAT . . .

The human body loses enough heat in an hour
to boil half a gallon of water.

If calcium is taken out of human bones, they
become so rubbery that they can be tied in a
knot like rope or string.

The city with the highest number of babies
born in taxis is New York, USA.

A giraffe has the same number of bones in its
neck as a human does.

Richard III of England, Louis XIV of France and
the Emperor Napoleon of France were all born
with teeth.

Fact Attack titles available from Macmillan

The prices shown below are correct at the time of going to press.
However, Macmillan Publishers reserve the right to show new retail prices
on covers which may differ from those previously advertised.

Awesome Aliens	**Ian Locke**	**£1.99**
Beastly Bodies	**Ian Locke**	**£1.99**
Crazy Creatures	**Ian Locke**	**£1.99**
Fantastic Football	**Ian Locke**	**£1.99**
Dastardly Deeds	**Ian Locke**	**£1.99**
Cool Cars	**Ian Locke**	**£1.99**
Mad Medicine	**Ian Locke**	**£1.99**
Gruesome Ghosts	**Ian Locke**	**£1.99**
Dreadful Disasters	**Ian Locke**	**£1.99**
Nutty Numbers	**Rowland Morgan**	**£1.99**

All Macmillan titles can be ordered at your local bookshop
or are available by post from:

**Book Service by Post
PO Box 29, Douglas, Isle of Man IM99 1BQ**

Credit cards accepted. For details:
Telephone: 01624 675137
Fax: 01624 670923
E-mail: bookshop@enterprise.net

Free postage and packing in the UK.
Overseas customers: add £1 per book (paperback)
and £3 per book (hardback).